FACING YOUR FEAR OF BEING ALONE

BY MARI SCHUH

PEBBLE
a capstone imprint

Published by Pebble, an imprint of Capstone.
1710 Roe Crest Drive, North Mankato, Minnesota 56003
capstonepub.com

Copyright © 2023 by Capstone. All rights reserved. No part of this publication may be reproduced in whole or in part, or stored in a retrieval system, or transmitted in any form or by any means, electronic, mechanical, photocopying, recording, or otherwise, without written permission of the publisher.

Library of Congress Cataloging-in-Publication Data is available on the Library of Congress website.
ISBN: 9780756570842 (hardcover)
ISBN: 9780756571252 (paperback)
ISBN: 9780756570941 (ebook PDF)

Summary: Explores the reasons why people are afraid of being alone and describes simple tips for facing this fear.

Editorial Credits
Editor: Erika L. Shores; Designer: Dina Her; Media Researcher: Jo Miller; Production Specialist: Tori Abraham

Image Credits
Getty Images: Amir Mukhtar, 10, Cavan Images, 14, danez, 17, FG Trade, 11, JGI/Tom Grill, 4, Noel Hendrickson, 15, Rebecca Nelson, 9; Shutterstock: Andrey Arkusha, 7, behindthemirror, 13, Daisy Daisy, 8, Domira (background), cover and throughout, Kapitosh (cloud), cover and throughout, Littlekidmoment, Cover, Marish (brave girl), cover and throughout, Pavel Kobysh, 19, RMC42, 5, Waridsara_HappyChildren, 6, Zalena Photo, 21

All internet sites appearing in back matter were available and accurate when this book was sent to press.

Printed and bound in China. PO5130

TABLE OF CONTENTS

Being Alone 4

Ways to Feel Better 8

Making Changes 14

Happy and Healthy 18

Take a Breathing Break 20

Glossary 22

Read More 23

Internet Sites 23

Index 24

About the Author 24

Words in **bold** are in the glossary.

BEING ALONE

Are you sometimes scared to be alone? Maybe you don't like to play alone or sleep alone. Just thinking about it might make you worry. But facing your fears can help make it easier.

It's OK to be scared of being alone. It's a normal **emotion**. Many kids have this fear at times. Grown-ups sometimes feel this way too.

When you feel scared, your mind and body feel **stress**. Your thoughts might race. It can be hard to **focus** on other things. You might cry, shake, or sweat. Your stomach or head can hurt. Your heart might beat quickly. It could be hard to go to sleep.

These feelings are not fun. But there is good news. You can learn to **relax** your mind and body. Then you will feel **calm**.

WAYS TO FEEL BETTER

When you are scared of being alone, be **mindful** of your breath. Slow, deep breaths can relax your mind and body. It can lessen your feelings of fear.

If you are afraid of sleeping alone, a **routine** at bedtime can help. Listen to music or read a book. Keep your door open. Use a night-light. Sleep with a toy or blanket you like. Do things that will make you feel safe.

Talking can help you face your fear of being alone. Talk about your feelings with someone you trust. They will listen and help. Do you have a favorite doll or stuffed animal? Tell it your fears. Talk to yourself out loud too. Tell yourself that you will be OK.

A warm hug can relax you. Or ask someone you trust to hold your hand.

You might feel like trying to never be alone. Lots of people feel like that. But **avoiding** being alone does not get rid of your fear. It does not make you feel calm.

Instead, you can **practice** being alone. Learning to be alone takes time. So be patient with yourself. You can start to practice when you are ready.

MAKING CHANGES

Small changes can help you face your fear. If you don't like playing alone in your room, keep the door open. Then you can hear your family in the other room.

Play alone for a few minutes. How did you feel? Next time, play alone for a longer time.

15

Playing alone can be fun. Find a special place just for you. Gather your favorite toys and books. Turn off your devices. Build a fort. Listen to music as you play. Or find a spot to play outdoors.

HAPPY AND HEALTHY

Sometimes you might still feel afraid of being alone. That's OK. You can have **confidence** as you face your fears. You can learn to think in a positive way. It will be easier to deal with your feelings. Then you will feel happy and healthy.

TAKE A BREATHING BREAK

Do this activity to practice deep breathing. Then you will know how to relax your mind and body when you are scared of being alone. When you know how to help yourself feel better, then it's easier to be alone.

What You Need

- pencil, crayon, or marker
- notebook or paper

What You Do

1. Draw some big mountains on a piece of paper. You can make them look like the letter M.

2. Next, trace over the shape of the mountains with your pointer finger. Breathe in when you climb up the mountain. Breathe out when you climb down.

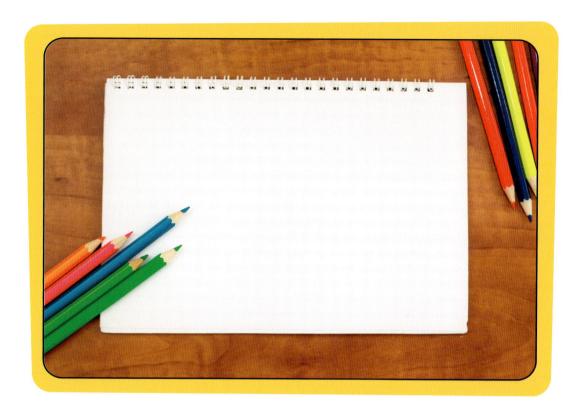

3. Breathe in and out slowly. Take deep breaths.

4. As you breathe, think of some good things about being alone. You might like having some quiet time away from people. You might like not having to share your toys with anyone. Remember a time when you enjoyed being alone.

5. Notice how your body feels. How did you feel at the start of the activity? How does your body feel now?

GLOSSARY

avoid (uh-VOYD)—to stay away from something

calm (KAHM)—quiet and peaceful

confidence (KON-fuh-duhns)—a feeling or belief that you can do well

emotion (i-MOH-shuhn)—a strong feeling; people have and show emotions such as happiness, sadness, fear, and anger

focus (FOH-kuss)—to keep all your attention on one thing

mindful (MIND-full)—being aware of your body, mind, and feelings in the present moment

practice (PRAK-tiss)—to keep working to get better at a skill

relax (reh-LAKS)—to calm down

routine (roo-TEEN)—a set of tasks done in a set order

stress (STRESS)—worry, strain, or pressure

READ MORE

Borgert-Spaniol, Megan. *Friends Support Each Other.* North Mankato, MN: Pebble, an imprint of Capstone, 2022.

McAneney, Caitie. *Sometimes We Feel Afraid.* New York: Cavendish Square Publishing, 2022.

Wilson, Lakita. *Sometimes I Feel Lonely.* North Mankato, MN: Pebble, an imprint of Capstone, 2022.

INTERNET SITES

Fear Facts for Kids
kids.kiddle.co/Fear

Feelings Worksheet
kids-pages.com/folders/worksheets/Feelings/page2.htm

Kids Talk About: Feeling Scared
kidshealth.org/en/kids/comments-scared.html

INDEX

avoiding, 12

confidence, 18

emotions, 4

feelings, 6, 7, 8, 10, 18

mindfulness, 8

playing, 4, 14, 16

practice, 12

routines, 8

sleeping, 4, 6, 8

stress, 6

ABOUT THE AUTHOR

Mari Schuh's love of reading began with cereal boxes at the kitchen table. Today she is the author of hundreds of nonfiction books for beginning readers. Mari lives in the Midwest with her husband and their sassy house rabbit. Learn more about her at marischuh.com.